SCHIRMER'S LIBRARY OF MUSICAL CLASSICS

Vol. 328

JACQUES DONT

Op. 37

Twenty-Four Exercises

For the Violin

Preparatory to the Studies of

R. KREUTZER and P. RODE

Edited and Fingered by

LOUIS SVEČENSKI

⊕

ISBN 978-0-7935-5678-6

G. SCHIRMER, Inc.

DISTRIBUTED BY

7777 W. BLUEMOUND RD. P.O. BOX 13819 MILWAUKEE, WI 53213

PREFACE

In using Hans Wessely's edition of the Kreutzer Études, and the special exercises by Franz Kneisel ("Advanced Exercises for the Violin"), I have found that a great many students experience difficulty in carrying out the excellent instructions therein given for acquiring a correct position of the left hand (retaining the fingers in their places), owing to insufficient attention to the correct placing of the fingers during the years of elementary and preparatory study.

Students who follow faithfully the instructions given in this edition of Dont's Studies will find themselves repaid—when ready to take up the Kreutzer Études—by having acquired the correct position of the left hand, without which a reliable technic cannot be attained.

LOUIS SVEČENSKI.

12153

Preparatory Exercises

to the Studies of

R. Kreutzer and P. Rode

Λ Up-bow
⊔ Down-bow

**Edited and fingered by
Louis Svečenski**

Notes marked ◇ indicate place for "preparatory finger,"
and should not be sounded.
The length of the lines following finger-marks indicates
the time during which fingers should retain their places.

Jacques Dont. Op. 37

*) Use the entire length of the bow when played slowly, only the half when quickly.

Allegro

2.

poco ritard.

Allegretto

3.

5th Pos.

6

*) Half-bow for the slurred notes in slow or moderato tempo; diminish the length when played quickly.

8

*) See Note to N⁰ 4.

12158

Vivace

7.

Andante con moto

8.

p ben legato

For the bowing, see Foot-note*)

9.

*) { From A to B with a third of the bow } at the point.
{ From B to C with a third of the bow } in the middle.
{ From C to D with a third of the bow } at the nut.

12153

14

For practice of the Mordente and Appoggiatura.

Allegro commodo.

11.

Vivace

12. *)

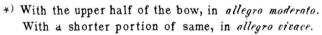

*) With the upper half of the bow, in *allegro moderato*.
With a shorter portion of same, in *allegro vivace*.

18

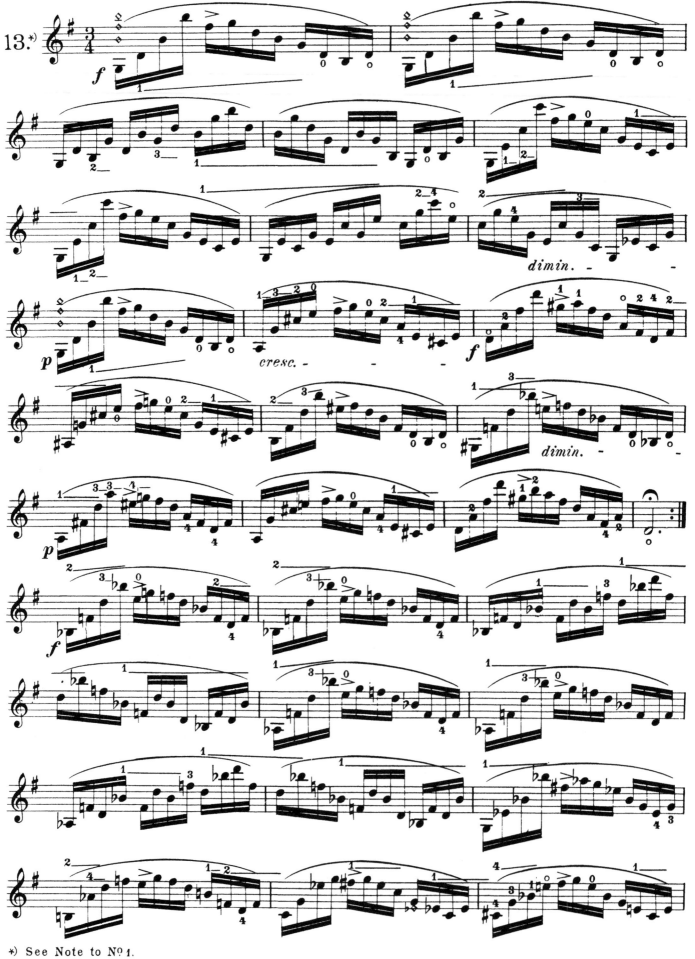

13.

Allegro non troppo

14.

Allegro moderato

15.

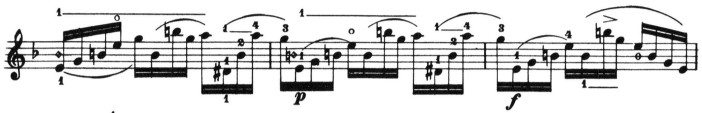

Allegretto agitato

16.

Andante con moto

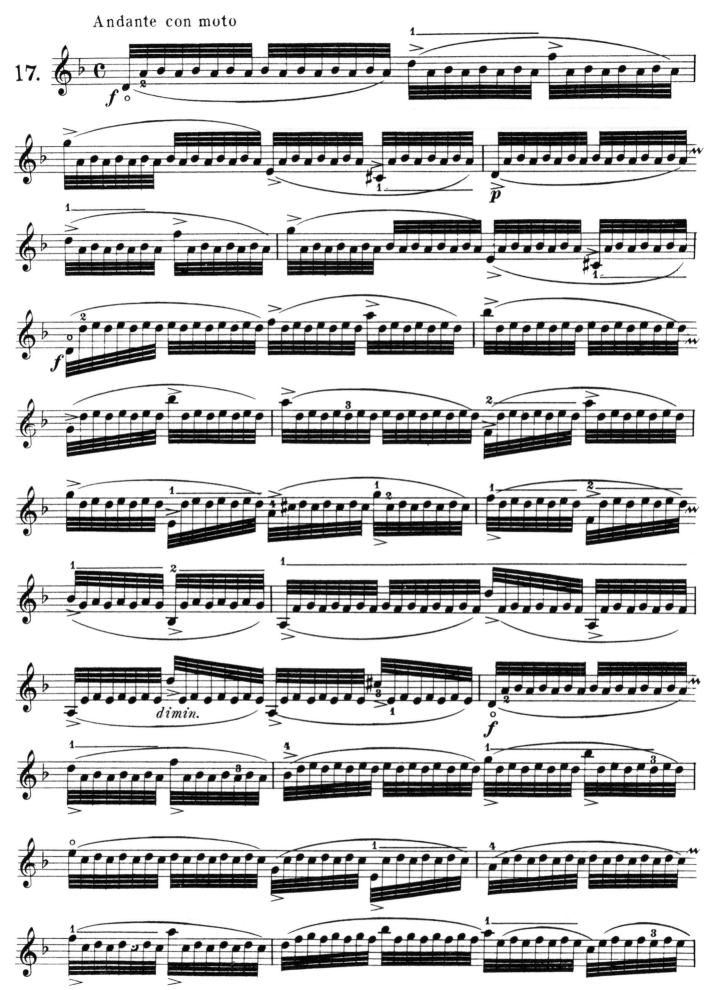

17.

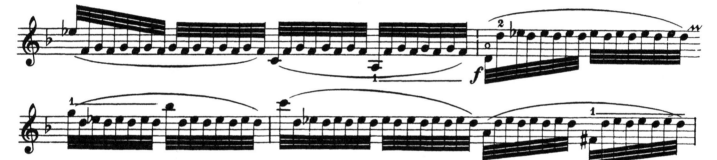

dimin.

morendo

12158

For practice in double-stopping with marked and detached bowing.

Allegro

18.

dimin. e poco rallent.

Andante

19.

Allegretto vivo

20.

Allegro assai

21.

Vivace